Be Good to Your Body

Healthy Eating & Fun Recipes

Roz Fulcher

Dover Publications, Inc.
Mineola, New York

Bibliographical Note

Be Good to Your Body—Healthy Eating and Fun Recipes is a
new work, first published by Dover Publications, Inc., in 2012.

International Standard Book Number
ISBN-13: 978-0-486-48643-7
ISBN-10: 0-486-48643-5

Manufactured in the United States by LSC Communications
4500052366
www.doverpublications.com

NOTE

Healthy eating is easy—and fun, too! In this handy book, you'll learn about healthy foods and also find out how to prepare meals and snacks that are full of healthful and tasty ingredients. Make your own fish tacos, sandwich kebobs, frozen pops, and "yogurt-cicles." Create breakfast bars packed with nutrients, and try your hand at porcupine balls, muesli, ants on a log, gorp, and even a "power pancake." There's lots of information about vitamins and other good things that you can easily make a part of your everyday eating. First up: 6-Minute Healthy Potato Chips!

Before you start any of these recipes, please let an adult know so that he or she can supervise. Many of the recipes involve slicing the ingredients, using a stove, or operating a blender—all of which can be dangerous. **<u>Make sure that the adult helper is by your side in the kitchen as you prepare the recipes!</u>**

Be Good to Your Body

Healthy Eating & Fun Recipes

6-Minute Healthy Potato Chips

Ingredients:

1 russet potato
non-stick cooking spray
glass plate (or parchment paper)
seasoning of choice

Cut a piece of parchment paper (or use a glass plate). Have a helper slice 1/3 of a russet potato in paper-thin slices using a sharp knife, mandoline or peeler. Place slices on plate in a single layer and spray with your non-stick cooking spray. Season to taste and heat in microwave for 6 minutes on "high".

Results may vary depending on your microwave. You want them to be lightly golden. Repeat the process until you have used your entire potato.
Enjoy!

Russet potatoes are a rich source of fiber, potassium and vitamin C

15 Bean Soup

Soak dry beans in a large pan of water overnight or for at least 8 hours. Drain beans and replace with 2 quarts water and add ham hocks. Bring to a boil and reduce heat. Simmer for 2 hours uncovered. After simmering, add onions, tomatoes, chili powder, lemon juice and garlic. Serve with cornbread.

Beans are low in a fat but high in protein and soluble fiber. This makes them a great source for energy and nutrition.

Ingredients:

1 15oz can stewed or diced tomatoes

1 tsp chili powder

1 20 oz bag 15 beans for soup

1 lb. of ham hocks

1 cup chopped onion

1 clove minced garlic

juice of 1 lemon

Ants on a Log

1. Wash celery and cut into 5-inch lengths.
2. Spread organic peanut butter in the u-shaped part of the celery from one end to the other.
3. Press raisins into the peanut butter.

Other variations:

Gnats on a log- Replace raisins with currants.
Ladybugs on a log- Replace raisins with dried cranberries.
Ants on vacation- No raisins.
Ants on a snowy log- Replace peanut butter with low fat cream cheese.

Celery is rich in vitamin C.

Celery also lowers cholesterol and reduces high blood pressure.

Bag o' Bugs

Place graham crackers in a plastic bag and seal it shut. Crush crackers into a fine sand by using a large spoon or rolling pin. Add dried fruits and sugar-free gummy worms to your "soil".
Dig through with a spoon to catch your bugs and eat 'em!

Dried fruits are a sweet treat that are a good source of fiber. They contain vital vitamins and minerals such as Vitamins C, A, B6, Potassium and Magnesium.

You will need:

2 graham cracker sheets
raisins (ants)
dried cranberries (ladybugs)
currants (beetles)
sugar-free gummy worms
sealable plastic bag
heavy spoon

The Bell Pepper
Stuffed Bell Peppers

4 large bell peppers
1 lb lean organic ground beef
1 small onion chopped
1 1/2 cups tomato sauce

1/2 tsp sea salt
2 tbsp worcestershire sauce
1 cup cooked brown rice
1 cup low fat shredded cheese

Preheat oven to 375 degrees. Cut tops off of peppers and remove seeds. Place hollowed peppers in a baking dish coated with non stick spray. Set aside and heat 2 tspns of olive oil in a large skillet and brown beef. Drain fat and add diced onion. Saute for 3 minutes. Add salt, pepper, w. sauce, half the cheese and rice. Cook for 2 minutes to warm through. Remove from heat and spoon mixture into hollowed peppers. Pour tomato sauce into the baking dish. Cover with foil and bake for 45 minutes. Remove foil, top with remaining cheese and cook an additional 15 minutes.

5

Breakfast Bars

<u>No Bake Honey Bars</u>

1 1/2 cups peanut butter
1 cup honey
5 cups dry cereal

3/4 cup brown sugar (optional)
1/2 cup dried fruit and/or nuts

Combine pb, honey and brown sugar in a sauce pan. Bring to a boil, stirring constantly. Remove from heat and add remaining ingredients. Mix well. Use a greased spatula to press mixture into a 9" x 12" x 2" pan. Let cool and cut into squares.

Breakfast Bar

1/2 cup whole wheat flour 1/4 cup apple sauce
1/2 cup rolled oats   3 tbsp honey
1/2 tsp baking soda   1/2 tsp vanilla extract
1/4 tsp cinnamon   1/2 cup dried fruit
1/4 cup olive oil   non-stick cooking spray

By making your own energy/breakfast bars, you can cut out a lot of preservatives and artificial flavorings.

Spray 8"x8"x2" baking dish with nonstick spray. In a bowl combine flour, oats, baking soda, cinnamon and set aside. In another bowl, mix oil, apple sauce, honey and vanilla extract. Stir wet ingredients into the flour. Stir in fruit bits and spread mixture into pan. Bake at 350 for 15 to 20 minutes until toothpick comes out clean. Cool and cut into bars.

Blender Soups

Here's a fun way to create a delicious and easy soup using your favorite vegetables and a blender. This recipe calls for broccoli but carrots, asparagus, cauliflower, squash and parsnips work great as well. Try combining veggies for another taste experience.

Broccoli was developed in Italy and is recognized as an anti-cancer food.

Break broccoli up into "florets" and place into a pot. Add water and salt. Boil until soft (about 20 minutes).

Have an adult helper ladle slightly cooled broccoli and water into a blender.

Blend until thick and smooth.

Pour soup into bowls and add a small nob of organic butter. Add pepper to taste.

You will need:

2 "bundles" of broccoli
3 cups water
1 tsp sea salt
pepper to taste
organic butter (optional)

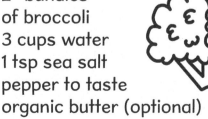

The Brussels Sprout

Ingredients:
A bag of fresh brussels sprouts
cleaned and outer leaves removed
2 tbsp olive or coconut oil
unrefined sea salt
fresh ground pepper

Brussels sprouts look like miniature heads of cabbage and are similar in taste but milder in flavor.

Preheat oven to 400 degrees.
Chop stems off of Brussels sprouts and slice each in half length wise. In a bowl mix oil, salt and pepper. Toss Brussels sprouts in oil mixture and spread onto a baking sheet. Roast in oven for about 20 minutes or until browned.
Remove from oven and serve as a sidedish.

Brussel sprouts were named after the capital of Belgium where it is believed they were first cultivated.

Campfire Treats

Baked Apples and Bananas

Bananas: Split banana lengthwise, leaving skin on. Insert peanut butter into the split. Wrap in foil and bake on coals (or grill) for 5 minutes. Allow to cool and serve with a spoon.

A backyard campout is a great way to spend a Fall or early Winter evening enjoying campfire treats.

peanut butter

butter

apples

brown sugar

cinnamon

tin foil

bananas

Carrot Patch Snack

You will need :

baby carrots
hummus
small paper cups
sprigs of parsley
toothpicks

For each "carrot patch", spoon 3 tablespoons of hummus into a small paper cup. Take 3 to 4 carrots and use a toothpick to poke a hole in the top of each one. Insert a sprig of parsley into each hole.
Take your carrots and "plant" them in the hummus.
For a fun presentation, place your cups into a mini terracotta pot that can be taken home to plant a little garden.

Carrots are root vegetables that originated in Afghanistan, but they were not orange.

In the 16th century, Dutch carrot growers invented the orange carrot by cross breeding yellow and red carrots.

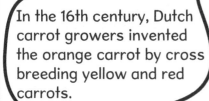

Chocolate Pretzels

1 12 oz package dark chocolate chips
1 tbsp coconut oil
1 bag of your favorite pretzels
(rods, twists, sticks)
Assorted sprinkles (opt.)

Line a baking sheet with wax paper. Place chocolate chips and shortening in a microwave-safe dish. Microwave on high for 30 second increments for about 1.5 minutes. Stir after each 30 seconds to prevent from burning. Carefully remove bowl and stir chocolate until smooth.

Dark chocolate contains more cocoa than other chocolates.

Cocoa is rich in flavonoids and contains a chemical - Epicatechin- known to help lower blood pressure.

Take each pretzel and dip half of it in the chocolate mix and place on wax paper. Leave space between each pretzel. Place in fridge for 30 minutes to harden chocolate. If using sprinkles, add while chocolate is still soft so that they will stick.

PRETZELS

Chicken Nuggets

You will need:

2 halved boneless/skinless
chicken breasts cut into chunks
1 cup natural bread crumbs

1 cup corn flakes
3 egg whites
1 teaspoon sea salt

1. Preheat oven to 375 degrees.
Place cornflakes in a plastic bag
and crush finely with a rolling pin.
Mix crushed cornflakes with
bread crumbs and salt in a shallow bowl.

2. In another bowl, whisk
egg whites. Coat each chicken
chunk lightly in egg mixture.

Corn
flakes

Bread

Most supermarket chicken nuggets are full of additives or processed meats. They are usually cooked in hydrogenated vegetable oil and trans fats.

Create your own crumbs by adding 2 slices of bread to a blender or food processor and "whiz" until fine.

3. Next, dip into bread crumbs, coating evenly. Place nuggets on lightly greased baking tray and bake for 20 minutes or until golden and cooked through.

Honey Mustard Dipping Sauce

1 tablespoon Dijon mustard
1 1/2 teaspoons honey
Mix ingredients and serve with nuggets.

Creamy Crab Soup

You will need:

1/2 cup butter
1/2 cup all purpose flour
1 to 2 tbsp seafood seasoning
1/2 teaspoon curry powder
4 cups organic milk
1 pound fresh crabmeat or
3 cans (6 oz each) crabmeat drained, flaked and cartilage removed.
2 tbsp minced fresh parsley

If a crab loses its claw, it grows back.

Melt butter in a 3-quart saucepan. Stir in flour, seafood seasoning, salt and curry powder. Cook until thick and bubbly. Gradually add milk and whisk until mixture is hot but DO NOT boil.

Add crabmeat to soup. Stir in parsley. Cook and stir just until crab is heated through. If too thick, thin soup with additional milk. Garnish with parsley.

Cucumber Yogurt Boats

Halve cucumbers lengthwise and scoop out the seeds. A melon baller works well for this. Mix low-fat plain yogurt with sugar, salt and cumin. Spread into hollowed cucumbers and serve.

Ingredients:

small cucumbers
1 cup plain low-fat yogurt
1/2 tsp raw sugar
1/8 tsp salt
a dash of cumin
(roughly 1/16 tsp)

Egg in a Nest

Use a biscuit cutter (or glass) to cut a hole in the center of your slice of bread. Coat bottom of non-stick pan with olive oil and heat to medium heat. Place your slice of bread in the pan and break an egg into the hole. When the white of egg is set, flip the bread over with a wide spatula. Continue cooking until egg is firm. Remove from pan and sprinkle with grated cheese (opt.)

Eggs are the only foods that contain naturally occuring vitamin D.

Ingredients:

olive oil

eggs

Bread

bread of choice

Dipping Fun

Carrots with Peanut Sauce

In a bowl, mix all ingredients together with a fork or whisk.
Add water as needed to make sauce smooth. Serve with
carrot sticks. Apple slices and celery also go well with this sauce.

Storing carrots in water keeps them crisp and juicy.

carrot sticks

3 tablespoons of all-natural peanut butter

a splash of low sodium soy sauce

A few drops of sesame oil

1 tablespoon honey

Cherries with Brown Sugar Dip

In a bowl stir sour cream (or yogurt) together with brown sugar and cinnamon. Rinse cherries and serve with your dip. Strawberries also work well with this dip.

The cherry stems make for easy dipping.

1 tablespoon brown sugar

1/4 teaspoon cinnamon

1/4 cup yogurt or low fat sour cream

cherries with stems attached

Eggs

Eggs are a good source of high-quality protein, which helps supply the amino acids our bodies need. Eggs also provide an important nutrient called "Choline" which is important for brain function.

Organic eggs from free range birds are recommended for the best health benefits from eating eggs.

Easy Omelette

3 organic eggs
2 tbsp low fat milk
handful of chopped ham
1/2 chopped green onion
1 cup shredded low fat cheese

Place milk and eggs into a bowl and whisk well. Add all ingredients and give it a good stir.

Grease a pan with olive oil and set to a high heat and pour in egg mixture.

When edges are cooked, fold in half with a spatula. Heat for another couple of minutes and then serve.

Fizzy Fruit Slushie

1. Combine juice and cut fruit and place in a glass baking dish, cover and freeze for at least 6-8 hours.

2. Remove from freezer and let stand at room temperature for 10-15 minutes. With a spoon scrape mixture to make a slush.

3. Fill glasses half full and top with seltzer. Top with a fruit wedge and serve with a spoon.

Most fruit juices are a good source of potassium which helps regulate blood pressure.

1 cup chopped pineapple

club Soda

chilled club soda

1 tbsp lime juice

2 cups orange juice

1 banana chopped

1 cup chopped mango

1 cup pineapple juice

Fish Tacos

1 lb white fish (tilapia, cod, halibut)
lime pepper seasoning
12- 24 fresh corn tortillas
low-sodium salsa (optional)

4 cups shredded red cabbage
1 lime cut into wedges
cilantro for garnish

Fish are loaded with Omega 3 fatty acids which protect from heart disease and are a great brain food.

Sprinkle fish with lime pepper and pan fry in a non-stick skillet on medium heat until cooked through - about 5 minutes on each side. With a little bit of olive oil, heat corn tortillas on a hot griddle until warm and softened.

Creamy Taco Sauce:
3/4 cup low fat mayo
3/4 cup plain yogurt
1 tsp seafood seasoning
juice of 1 lime
**Mix ingredients
and refrigerate.**

For each taco, place shredded fish on 2 overlapping tortillas.
Top with cabbage and a generous spoonful of cream sauce.
Add a spoon of low-sodium salsa, a squeeze of lime juice
and sprinkle with cilantro. Fold taco in half and enjoy.

Flavored Water

Take a plain jug of ice water and turn it into an exciting beverage, perfect for a hot summer day.

Ideas:
*Slice strawberries or mash raspberries with a fork and add to jug.
*Scrunch (bruise) mint leaves and toss in water along with sliced lemons or limes.
*Add sliced cucumbers to water for a refreshing taste.

Water is crucial to your health. It makes up 60% of your body weight.

Drink lots of water!

27

Frozen Grape Pops

These make a perfect treat on a hot day. Wash your grapes and pat dry with a paper towel. Carefully slide your grapes (about 4-6) onto a lollipop stick. Place your grape sticks in a plastic baggie and freeze for at least an hour. Pineapple chunks and blueberries also work well for this frozen treat.

Grapes are said to be the oldest cultivated fruit.

Grapes are a rare fruit that are completely cholesterol free.

You will need:

seedless grapes

lollipop sticks

freezer bag

Yogurt-cicles

Here is a simple but delicious way to eat yogurt on a hot summery day. Gently spoon your favorite yogurt into paper cups and cover with plastic wrap. Insert a popsicle stick (or spoon) through the wrap. Place in a freezer for several hours to harden.

Most yogurts contain "good for you" bacteria called **Probiotics**.

Probiotics are beneficial bugs that live in your digestive tract and help crowd out harmful microorganisms.

You will need:

2 cups organic low-fat flavored yogurt
small paper cups
popsicle sticks
1 cup assorted berries (optional)

Fun Fruit Pizza

Recipe:

1. Preheat oven to 350 degrees.
2. Take cream cheese out of fridge to soften.
3. Place cookie dough on nonstick cookie sheet and press 1/4" thick.
4. Bake 15-20 minutes or until golden brown.

5. Wash and slice fruit while cookie is baking.
6. After cookie dough has cooled, spred cream cheese mixture on top of cookie
7. Arrange fruit slices on top of cream cheese mixture in a fun pattern.

An egg slicer is a great tool for slicing kiwis and strawberries.

Ingredients:

4 cups assorted fruit (blueberries, raspberries, strawberries, kiwi fruit, bananas- or fruits of your choice).

18 oz. ready made cookie dough

8 oz low-fat cream cheese

Kiwi Fruit

Did you know that the kiwi fruit is more than 700 years old? It tastes like a mix between banana, pineapple and strawberry.

Whole Wheat Cookie Crust

1 cup (2 sticks) softened butter
1/4 cup sugar
2 cups white whole wheat flour

Cream butter and sugar. Stir in flour and finish with your hands. It may seem too crumbly at first but stick with it and it will form together. Continue with #3 of recipe.

Sugar

1/3 cup sugar
(optional)

Garlic

Roasted Garlic

Preheat oven to 375 degrees. Take a few heads of garlic and cut 1/2" off the top of the heads. Peel off any loose papery skin. Place garlic in a small baking dish cut side up. Drizzle 1 teaspoon of olive oil over the top of each bulb and let it sink in between the cloves. Cover with tin foil and bake for 45 minutes. Cloves will be brown on tips and soft throughout. Roasted garlic loses its sharp bite and turns into a sweet, mellow flavor.

Eat directly from the clove pockets or squeeze out like a paste. Spread on crusty bread drizzled with olive oil or give it a try mixed in mashed potatoes- yum!

Garlic is widely used around the world for its pungent flavor as a seasoning or condiment.

Gorp

Basic Mix:

Equal parts nuts and raisins with a small addition of pretzels and chocolate morsels.

This trail mix is ideal for long hikes because it replenishes calories on active days. It is also a healthy choice for road trips.

Gummi Candies

In a small saucepan, combine both the flavored and unflavored gelatin mixes. Pour cold water into the pan and stir with a spatula until you have a pastelike consistency. Heat pan on medium-low to melt paste, stirring until mixture is dissolved and you have a more waterlike texture. Pour mixture into a miniature candy mold of your choice. Place mold in freezer for 10 minutes to firm your gummi candy. Remove from freezer and enjoy.

Gelatin is made from a product found naturally in the collagen of animals. Gelatin is known to improve one's skin, hair and nail health.

You will need:

1/2 cup cold water

1 3oz package sugar-free flavored gelatin.

6 packets of unflavored gelatin

⊂Sandwich Kebob⊃

Have fun recreating your favorite lunchtime sandwich into a kebob. Have an adult helper cube bread, cheese, meat and vegetables into bite-sized pieces. Carefully "thread" onto a wooden skewer.

Shish-Kebob:
A dish consisting of small chunks of meat placed on skewers alternately with tomatoes, onions and green peppers.

A low fat mayo or dressing makes a great dip for your kebob.

Macaroni Bake

Ingredients:
4 oz multi-grain macaroni
3 tblspns olive oil
3 tblspns whole wheat bread crumbs
1/2 tspn sea salt
1/8 tspn pepper
2 cups lowfat skim milk
1/2 cup shredded low fat cheddar cheese

Mac & cheese is a **comfort food** favorite.

"Comfort food" is food that when eaten gives a sense of well being.

Preheat oven to 350 degrees. Coat an 8x8 baking dish with non-stick spray. Cook macaroni according to package directions. Place olive oil in a large sauce pan on medium heat. Add flour, paprika, salt and pepper. Add milk, whisking constantly. Continue cooking and stirring for 5 minutes until thickened. Stir in cheese and when it is melted, add macaroni coating evenly. Pour into the baking dish and top with bread crumbs. Bake for 15 minutes until hot and bubbly.

Muesli

Muesli is a cereal made from whole oats, nuts and dried fruit. It is high in dietary fiber, protein and healthy sugars.

To prepare a good muesli build your mixture as follows:
80% grains
10% nuts and seeds
10% dried fruit

Store your muesli in an airtight container such as a glass jar with a secure lid. Prepare enough for 2 weeks.

Muesli is from the Swiss-German word "Mus", which means mixture.

nuts and seeds: unsalted sunflower seeds, walnuts, cashews, almonds

dried fruits: apples, currants, dates, raisins

grains: rolled oats or wheat flakes are the most common base for a muesli.

oats

Muesli

MILK

Party Potion 'N Mix

Potion

2 cups unrefined sugar
2 quarts water
2 envelopes of lime
    drink packet
1 quart gingerale
1 large can of pineapple juice

Mix all
ingredients in a large
punch bowl.

Pineapple juice reduces excess water build-up. It is high in Vitamin C.

Party Mix

1 cup toasted cereal (wheat, corn or oats)
1 cup goldfish crackers (or cheese crackers)
1 cup dried cranberries
1 cup cashews or favorite nuts
1 cup dark chocolate chips
1 cup miniature pretzel twists or sticks

This mix is lower in sodium and fat than traditional baked chex mixes.

Take all ingredients and mix into a large bowl.

Pizza Pie

Pizza Dough

1. In a large bowl mix water, salt and sugar until dissolved. Add oil then two cups of flour, stirring well. Add remaining flour and stir until a ball forms. Place ball of dough on a floured surface and press into a circle. Sprinkle yeast evenly over dough and "knead" for 5-10 minutes. Form into a ball again and place into a bowl coated in olive oil. Cover bowl with plastic wrap and leave at room temperature for 1 - 2 hours.

2. Divide dough into two sections, Roll on a floured surface to 1/4" thick. Form a circle or a square and place on a baking sheet lightly oiled and sprinkled with corn meal.

Ingredients
1 1/2 cups warm water
4 1/2 cups whole wheat flour
1 tblspn olive oil
2 1/2 tspn salt
1/2 tspn yeast

3.Spread tomato sauce evenly over dough.
Add cheese then add your favorite toppings.
Cook for 10 -15 minutes in a 450 degree oven.

Pizza originated
with the Greeks in the 16th
century. They baked
flatbreads topped with
oil, herbs, spices and dates.

Tomato Sauce and Toppings

1/2 cup fresh tomato or
marinara sauce (3 - 4 ounces)
sliced mozzarella cheese

Topping Suggestions:
black olives, mushrooms,
ham, green peppers, zucchini,
broccoli, spinach, pineapple

Flour

No-Bake Cookies

8 whole wheat graham cracker squares
1/4 cup raisins
1/4 cup organic peanut butter
2 1/2 tablespoons honey
4 teaspoons unsweetened coconut

1. Crush graham crackers in a plastic baggy with a big spoon or rolling pin until fine.

2. Combine crackers, raisins, peanut butter and honey into a small bowl.

3. Pat small balls of "dough" into cookie shapes and dredge in shredded coconut.

These no-bake cookies are high in fiber, protein and potassium.

Replace shredded coconut with shaved chocolate and chill in the fridge as an alternative.

The Pomegranate

The Pomegranate is a unique fruit, native to Iran, with a sweet and tart flavor.

To get the seeds without spattering red juice everywhere, have an adult helper "score" the pomegranate in half and submerge in cool water. Pry out seeds in handfuls and transfer to another bowl or paper towel to dry.

The seeds are edible and considered good roughage to help cleanse the body.

Two essential minerals from the pomegranate are potassium and manganese.

Each pomegranate is composed of multiple seeds that are surrounded by a sac of juice.

You can eat the fruit by chewing on the seeds to release the juice from the sacs and then swallow the seeds. Or you can chew the juice-filled sacs and spit out the seed.

Popcorn!

Popcorn is a healthy whole grain, low in fat treat. Try these fun flavors on this great snack.

Chili Popcorn

2 tbsp organic butter
1 tbsp dijon mustard
2 tsp chili powder
1/4 tsp sea salt
1/4 tsp ground cumin

Peanut Popcorn

1 cup roasted peanuts
1/4 cup organic butter
1 tbsp natural peanut butter
2 tsp sea salt

Sugar and Spice Popcorn

2 tbsp unrefined sugar
1/4 tsp cinnamon
1/4 tsp nutmeg
1/3 cup organic butter

For each recipe, begin by melting butter (and any other wet ingredients) over moderate heat. Drizzle over popcorn and sprinkle with dry ingredients.

Use about 5-6 cups of airpopped corn for the base of these recipes.

Popcorn is high in antioxidants, especially "Polyphenols". Polyphenols are the same compounds that give olive oil, chocolate and tea their beneficial properties.

45

Porcupine Balls

In a big bowl, combine lean ground beef, rice, Italian seasoning and onion. Mix ingredients with hands and form into golf-sized balls. Disposable clear plastic gloves are a good idea when working with raw meat.
Place meatballs into a large baking dish.

Brown rice is unprocessed white rice. It still contains the bran and germ which contain valuable nutrients.

A teaspoon of sugar added to tomato sauce reduces bitterness.

Mix tomato sauce and water and pour over your meatballs. Cover tightly with foil and bake in a 350 degree over for 1 hour. The rice will puff up, making your meatballs look like porcupines!

1 10.5 oz can of tomato sauce

1lb. Lean ground beef

1/2 cup long grain brown rice

1/2 cup chopped onion

1 teaspoon Italian herb seasoning

1/2 cup water

The Power Pancake

These "cakes" are jampacked with protein and fiber.

Ingredients:

1 cup 100% rolled oats
10 egg whites or 1 small
carton of egg whites
grapeseed oil
berries (fresh or frozen)
dash cinnamon sugar

Mix together oatmeal and egg whites in a bowl. Coat the bottom of a large frying pan with oil. Pour oat mixture into pan and cook at moderate heat. Pour as one large pancake that can be cut into wedges or individual servings. While bottom layer is cooking, sprinkle berries on top letting them sink in. When edges are slightly browned, flip cake over and continue cooking on other side until cooked. Sprinkle with cinnamon sugar if desired.

Oatmeal is the only whole grain that is recognized by the USFDA to help reduce cholesterol and reduce the risk of heart disease.

Roasted Pumpkin Seeds

Toasted pumpkin seeds have a nutty flavor.

1. Scoop seeds out and rinse under cold water, pulling off pulp and strings. This is easiest to do before pulp hardens and dries.

2. Place pumpkin seeds in a single layer on an oiled baking sheet stirring to coat.

3. Sprinkle with sea salt and bake in a 325 degree oven for 25 minutes, stirring after 10 minutes. Let cool and store in an air-tight container.

Pumpkin seeds are a great source of Magnesium and are packed with protein.

Magnesium helps keep our bones strong. It also promotes healthy heart rhythms and nervous system function.

Salsa & Pita Chips

You will need:
5 -8 tomatoes
1 clove garlic
1-3 jalapenos
1/2 of a red onion
1 large green pepper
1 fresh bunch of cilantro
sea salt

Salsa

Dice tomatoes, reserving juice. Chop remaining ingredients finely. Mix all ingredients into a bowl. Season with salt to taste. If you want a finer salsa, mix in blender to desired consistency. Refrigerate for one hour and serve.

"Salsa" is the Spanish and Italian word for sauce. The base of salsa is tomatoes which are rich in heart-healthy lycopenes.

Pita Chips

You will need:

12 pita bread pockets
1/2 cup olive oil
kosher salt

Preheat oven to 400 degrees.
Cut each pita into 8 triangles.
Place on lined cookie sheet.
In a small bowl, combine oil and
salt. Brush each triangle with mixture
and bake for 10 minutes or until pita
chips are slightly browned
and crispy.

Pita bread is
a leavened
flat bread. It
is created by
steam that puffs
up the dough.

Bean & Sausage Stew

Ingredients:

1 lb smoked turkey sausage
2 tbsp tomato paste
1 cup chopped onion
1 cup celery chopped
1 cup carrots chopped

1 16 oz chopped canned tomatoes
5 cups low-sodium chicken stock
1 cup Great Northern beans
1 cup red beans
2 cups zucchini cut into 1/2"-pieces
1 cup whole wheat bowtie pasta

A "stew" is a combo of ingredients that have been cooked in a liquid and served in the gravy that it creates.

Brown sausage in a skillet. Add tomato paste and cook 5 minutes. Add onions, celery, carrots and oregano. Cook another 5 minutes, add tomatoes and chicken stock. Stir in beans and zucchini. Bring to a boil and simmer for 30 minutes. Cook pasta separately. To serve, place pasta in a bowl and pour stew over the top.

Turkey sausage is lighter than regular sausage with fewer calories and fat grams.

Shake-a-Salad

Easy Bread Salad (Panzanella)

Instead of making salad in a bowl, make individual portions that go directly into a zipped plastic bag. The bag can be placed directly in a lunch box or taken on a picnic.

Panzanella is an Italian salad that always includes chewy bread, tomatoes and vegetables from the garden.

Begin by having an adult helper cube and dice ingredients for your bread salad. Place handfuls of each ingredient into your baggie. Drizzle with balsamic vinegar and extra virgin olive oil in the bag.

Seal the bag and ...

shake shake shake shake !

The basis of "salad" is sal (salt). In ancient times salt was often used in dressings to season raw vegetables.

Baggies

Root Veggie Mash

Boil 2 lbs of root vegetables in a pot of water for 20 minutes or until fork tender. Drain well and mash. Add organic butter or extra virgin olive oil to desired smooth consistency. Add salt and pepper to taste. Sprinkle with chopped parsley.

Root vegetables are plant roots that are edible. They are "tuberous", "stems" and "bulbs".

Root vegetables store energy in the form of the carbohydrates.

"SNIFF SNIFF"

extra virgin olive oil

parsnip

rutabaga

sweet potato

turnip

celery root

organic butter

parsley

Snack Cones

Edible serving containers make these a fun, no mess, no trash treat.

3 cups popcorn
2 cups multi grain cereal
1 cup dried fruit bits
24 wafer ice cream cones

Combine popcorn, cereal and dried fruit bits.
Scoop the mix into ice cream cones.

Multi grain cereal contains a variety of whole grains or grain flakes.

Typical grains used:
rice, corn, oats,
cracked rye,
barley, millet,
flax and soy.

Spicy Apple Cider

When English settlers came to the new world they brought cider apple seeds with them, which led to cider becoming one of America's most popular drinks.

Warm apple cider is an ideal treat on a Fall evening or cold Winter day.

In a large saucepan mix apple cider, allspice, honey and nutmeg. Place cinnamon sticks and cloves in a square of cheesecloth (or coffee filter) and tie with string. Add to cider. Bring to a boil, reduce and simmer mixture for 5 minutes. Transfer to a crockpot to keep warm and enjoy throughout the day. Remove cheesecloth and replace with orange slices. Serve with a stick of cinnamon.

Cheesy Spaghetti Squash

1. Cut squash in half and scoop out seeds and fibers. Place halves face down in a baking dish with enough water to cover bottom of dish. Bake in a 350° oven for 1 hour. Let cool for 15 minutes or until cool enough to handle.

2. Take a fork and scrape out the squash little by little. It will naturally separate into noodle-like strands. Toss squash gently with olive oil and parmesan cheese.

Ingredients:

1/4 cup olive oil

1 medium spaghetti squash

1/2 cup Parmesan cheese

Stir Fry

1 lb chicken breasts thinly sliced
2 tbsp sesame oil
4 cups fresh veggies- broccoli, green peppers,
onion, bean sprouts, zucchini, carrots, mushrooms..
1 1/2 cups chicken broth
3 tbsp soy sauce
3 tbsp cornstarch
2 tsp brown sugar
1 1/2 cups brown rice

At med-high heat, stir fry chicken
in sesame oil in large skillet or
"wok" until brown. Add vegetables
and cook until crisp-tender. In a bowl
mix broth, soy, starch and sugar. Add
to wok and continue cooking on high
heat for 2 minutes. Serve over
brown rice.

A "wok"
is a rounded-
bottom pot that
originated in China
and used often for
stir frying.

"Stir Fry" means
cooking food at
high heat while
stirring
constantly.

Stuffed French Toast

This recipe can be enjoyed for breakfast, lunch, brunch or even tossed in your lunchbox.

You will need:

2 slices sprouted grain bread
3 ounces egg whites
4 strawberries thinly sliced
2 ounces low fat mozzarella cheese
Maple or Agave syrup (optional)

Sprouted bread is made from whole grains that have been allowed to "sprout" -germinate- and is considered a "live" food.

"Is french toast French?"

1. Preheat a non-stick skillet over medium heat.
2. Put egg whites in a shallow bowl with a pinch of salt and sugar. Whisk slightly.
3. Layer a slice of bread with cheese and strawberry slices. Place 2nd slice on top
4. Carefully dip both sides of "sandwich" in egg whites.

"No. In England during the 1400's it was used to make stale bread moist and edible. The earliest mention of it is in a collection of Roman recipes during the 4th -5th century."

5. Place in a pan and cook for 2 minutes or until cheese is melting and bread is slightly crispy and brown.
6. Flip sandwich over. Reduce heat if needed and cook other side for another 1-2 minutes.
7. Remove from skillet and sprinkle cinammon, nutmeg, or powdered sugar. Serve with syrup if desired.

Sunflower Seeds

Sunflower seeds are ready for harvesting when the flower head is brown and dry. Most of the yellow petals have dried and fallen and the seeds will be plump. You can collect the seeds by tying a brown paper bag on the head and letting them drop naturally in the bag instead of the ground. Or you can rub the seeds out of the "head" by hand.

Sunflower seeds are the best whole food source of Vitamin E.

Cover unhulled seeds in salted water (2 quarts of water with 1/4 - 1/2 cups salt). Soak your seeds in the salt water overnight and drain on absorbent paper.

To roast sunflower seeds: Place a single layer of seeds in a shallow pan. Put pan in a 300° degree oven and roast for 30-40 minutes or until brown and crisp.

Sweet Potato Fries

 # Tea Time

In England, the tradition of "tea" was served around 4 or 5 o'clock. Most tea rooms serve hot tea with bread, butter and cakes.

Cheese & Pineapple Hedgehog

1 block of cheese
1 small pineapple
honeydew melon

Chop cheese and pineapple into bite-sized pieces and thread onto cocktail sticks. Halve a melon and place on plate, cut side down. Place cocktail sticks into melon until it resembles a hedgehog (also stick 2 blueberries for eyes and a grape for a nose to create a face.)

Very Berry Mint Tea

1/2 cup honey
2 mint-flavored tea bags
4 cups boiling water
1/2 cup fresh /frozen raspberries
mint sprigs for garnish (optional)

Place honey in a teapot, add teabags
and pour boiling water into pot. "Steep"
(let tea bags sit in water) for 5 minutes.
Remove tea bags.

Pour hot tea into pretty cups and place 2
to 3 raspberries into each cup.
Add a sprig of mint.

Cucumber Sandwiches

1 English cucumber
8 slices whole wheat or rye bread
2 tablespoons softened butter or light mayo
cherry tomatoes (optional)

Cut crusts off bread. If you like, use a cookie
cutter to create pretty-shaped sandwiches.
Spread each slice with a little bit of butter or
mayo and place a slice of cucumber on each.
If you didn't make shapes out of your bread,
cut your sandwiches into wedges or squares
for individual servings.

Mint tea is popular for strengthening
the immune system and for reducing
stress. This makes this herbal tea
a good choice for drinking before
bedtime.

The Apple

Apple Fondue

1/2 cup low-sugar chunky peanut butter
1/4 cup rice cereal
1/8 cup raisins or dried cranberries
2 apples cut into wedges

Mix peanut butter, cereal and raisins in a bowl. Dip apple wedges into peanut butter mixture.

The Onion

Baked Bloomin' Onion

Sauce:
1/2 cup lowfat
sour cream
2 tblspns ketchup
1/2 tspn sea salt
1/8 tspn cayenne pepper
1 1/2 tspn creamy horseradish
1/4 tspn paprika
Combine ingredients and serve with onion.

Onion:
1 large Vidalia onion
1/2 cup whole wheat
bread crumbs
2 egg whites beaten
1 tspn garlic powder
1 tspn paprika

Preheat oven to 375 degrees. Spray a baking sheet with nonstick spray. Peel onion and trim bottom so it sits flat. Cut onion into wedges, being sure not to cut through to the bottom, creating a flower effect. Place on baking sheet and pour whisked egg whites over onion and sprinkle with bread crumbs. Spray lightly with olive oil and bake for 40 - 50 minutes until onions are soft and browned on the tips. Serve with sauce.

Onions contain an oil which has a lot of sulphur in it. When cut, the oil gases reach your eye and cause irritation. Your tear glands produce tears to wash away the irritant.

Why do onions make you cry?

70

Turkey Joes

Ingredients:

1 1/2 lbs lean ground turkey
1 green bell pepper diced
1 medium onion diced
1/4 tspn sea salt

2 tblspns prepared mustard
3/4 cup low-sodium ketchup
2 tblspns raw sugar

Brown and drain turkey in a nonstick skillet. Add remaining ingredients and simmer for 20 minutes. Serve on whole wheat buns or rolls.

"Sloppy Joes" are an American sandwich typically made of ground beef and tomato sauce on a bun.

Ground turkey is a healthy alternative to ground beef.

Ground turkey has less calories than beef and less saturated fat.

sugar

Pickles

Twice-Baked Potato

Preheat oven to 375 degrees. Rub cleaned potatoes with olive oil and season with salt. Place on a baking sheet and bake for 1 hour. Remove from oven and let cool for 10 minutes.

Slice top off of each potato, scoop and place potato in a bowl and mash. Add low-fat sour cream (or yogurt), cheese, cooked broccoli and green onions. Evenly divide the mixture and refill potato shells and top with a little more shredded cheese. Place back in oven for 10-15 minutes.

Serve as a side dish or even as a main meal.

Ingredients:
1/2 cup low-fat sour cream
1 cup low-fat cheddar cheese
3 green onions
broccoli florets

4 medium russet potatoes
kosher salt
olive oil

Potatoes are a natural source for starch and carbohydrates.

A potato is 80% water and 20% solid.